P9-DNI-999

Under My Feet

Ants

Patricia Whitehouse

Heinemann Library
Chicago, Illinois

© 2004 Heinemann Library
a division of Reed Elsevier Inc.
Chicago, Illinois

Customer Service 888-454-2279
Visit our website at www.heinemannlibrary.com

Designed by Sue Emerson, Heinemann Library; Page layout by Que-Net Media™
Printed and bound in the United States by Lake Book Manufacturing, Inc.
Photo research by Bill Broyles

08 07 06 05 04
10 9 8 7 6 5 4 3 2 1

Library of Congress Cataloging-in-Publication Data
Whitehouse, Patricia, 1958-
  Ants / Patricia Whitehouse.
      v. cm. – (Under my feet)
Contents: Do ants live here? – What are ants? – What do ants look like? – Where do ants live? – What do ant homes look like? – How do ants find their way underground? – How do ants make their homes? – What is special about ant homes? – When do ants come out from underground? – Ant home map.
  ISBN 1-4034-4316-5 (HC), 1-4034-4325-4 (Pbk.)
  1. Ants–Juvenile literature. [1. Ants.] I. Title.
  QL568.F7W624 2003
  595.7′96–dc21

2003000035

Acknowledgments
The author and publishers are grateful to the following for permission to reproduce copyright material:
p. 4 James Frank/Stock Connection; p. 5 R. J. Erwin/DRK Photo; p. 6 Dale R. Thompson/Bruce Coleman Inc.; p. 7 Anthony Bannister/Gallo Images/Corbis; pp. 8, 10, 12 Dwight Kuhn; p. 9 Paul Beard/PhotoDisc; p. 11L Corbis; p. 11R C. McIntyre/PhotoLink/PhotoDisc; p. 13 Stephen P. Parker/Photo Researchers, Inc.; p. 14 Stephen J. Drasemann/DRK Photo; p. 15 Bahr/Premium Stock/PictureQuest; p. 16 Peter Ward/Bruce Coleman Inc.; p. 17 Panda/ FLPA; p. 18 John Shaw/Bruce Coleman Inc.; p. 19 D. Cavagnaro/DRK Photo; p. 19 Wolfgang Kaehler/Corbis; p. 20 Bruce Coleman Inc.; p. 21 Rudolf Freund/Photo Researchers, Inc.; p. 23 (row 1, L-R) Bahr/Premium Stock/PictureQuest, Anthony Bannister/ Gallo Images/Corbis, R. J. Erwin/DRK Photo; (row 2, L-R) Stephen P. Parker/Photo Researchers, Inc., Dale R. Thompson/ Bruce Coleman Inc., Dwight Kuhn; (row 3, L-R) Dwight Kuhn, Anthony Bannister/Gallo Images/Corbis; back cover (L-R) Bahr/Premium Stock/PictureQuest, Anthony Bannister/Gallo Images/Corbis

Illustration on page 22 by Will Hobbs
Cover photograph by Dwight Kuhn

Every effort has been made to contact copyright holders of any material reproduced in this book. Any omissions will be rectified in subsequent printings if notice is given to the publisher.

Special thanks to our advisory panel for their help in the preparation of this book:
Alice Bethke, Library Consultant
Palo Alto, CA

Eileen Day, Preschool Teacher
Chicago, IL

Kathleen Gilbert,
Second Grade Teacher
Round Rock, TX

Sandra Gilbert,
Library Media Specialist
Fiest Elementary School
Houston, TX

Jan Gobeille,
Kindergarten Teacher
Garfield Elementary
Oakland, CA

Angela Leeper,
Educational Consultant
Wake Forest, NC

Special thanks to Dr. William Shear, Department of Biology, Hampden-Sydney College, for his review of this book.

Some words are shown in bold, **like this.**
You can find them in the picture glossary on page 23.

Contents

Do Ants Live Here?

When you walk outside, you might not see an ant.

But you might be walking over one.

Some ants live under your feet.

Their homes are underground.

What Are Ants?

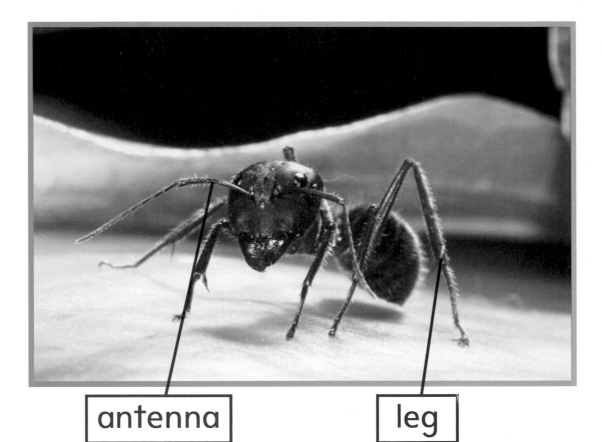

antenna

leg

Ants are **insects**.

Insects have six legs and two **antennae**.

exoskeleton

Ants and other insects have a hard outside.

It is called an **exoskeleton**.

What Do Ants Look Like?

head | body

Ants have a head and two body parts.

Most ants are black, but they can also be red or brown.

Ants are very small.

One ant could fit on the tip of your finger.

Where Do Ants Live?

Most ants live in underground **nests**.

They live together in a group called a **colony**.

You can find ants almost everywhere in the world.

What Do Ant Homes Look Like?

tunnel

Most ant **nests** have **tunnels.**

The tunnels lead to little rooms called **chambers.**

Each chamber has a special use.

There are chambers for food, for baby ants, and for resting.

How Do They Find Their Way?

antennae

Ants feel where they are going with their **antennae**.

You can see these ants tapping the ground.

Ants can also smell and taste with their antennae.

Smells and tastes let ants know where they are.

How Do Ants Make Their Homes?

mandibles

Ants shovel out dirt with their **mandibles**.

They carry the dirt outside.

Ants mix dirt with their spit to make **tunnel** walls.

The walls are hard when they are dry.

What Is Special About Their Homes?

Some ants make **nests** deep underground.

The nest stays warm during the cold winter.

Some ant nests are as big as your classroom.

A million ants can live there!

When Do Ants Come Out from Underground?

Ants leave the **nest** to find food.

They bring the food back to the nest.

Some ants might leave when the nest gets too crowded.

They will make a new nest.

Ant Home Map

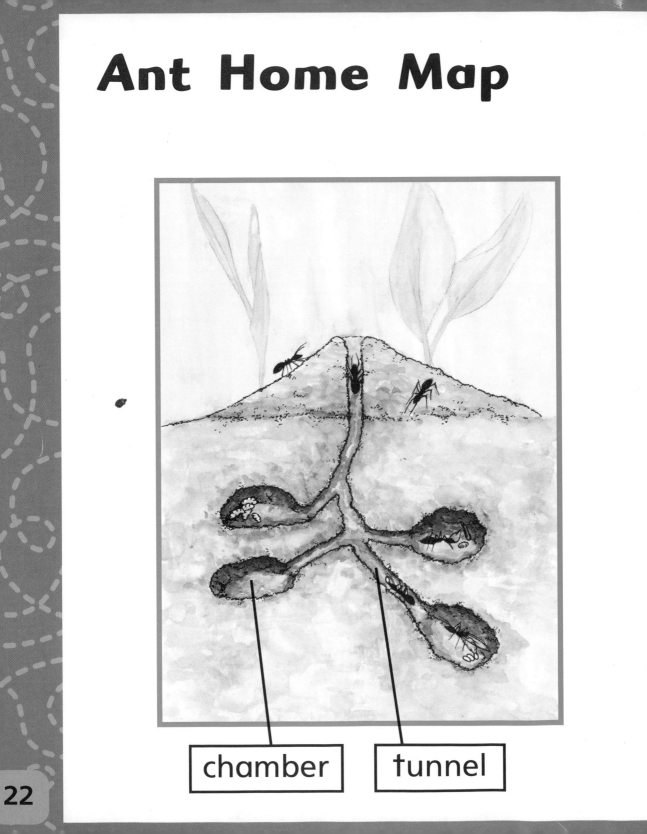

chamber   tunnel

Picture Glossary

antennae
pages 6, 14, 15

exoskeleton
page 7

nest
pages 10, 12,
18, 19, 20, 21

chamber
pages 12, 13, 22

insect
pages 6, 7

tunnel
pages 12, 17, 22

colony
page 10

mandibles
page 16

Note to Parents and Teachers

Reading for information is an important part of a child's literacy development. Learning begins with a question about something. Help children think of themselves as investigators and researchers by encouraging their questions about the world around them. Each chapter in this book begins with a question. Read the question together. Look at the pictures. Talk about what you think the answer might be. Then read the text to find out if your predictions were correct. Think of other questions you could ask about the topic, and discuss where you might find the answers. Assist children in using the picture glossary and the index to practice new vocabulary and research skills.

! CAUTION: Remind children that it is not a good idea to handle wild animals or insects. Children should wash their hands with soap and water after they touch any animal.

Index